New Shoes for Lilah

By Lillie Sheppard and Carol Core

Illustrations by Sudesha Shrestha and Deepak Thami

Cover and interior illustrations: Sudesha Shrestha and Deepak Thami
Book and Interior Design: Jane Doe Consulting
Editing: Jane Doe Consulting

Printed in the United States of America
First Printing, 2018

ISBN 978-0-9961998-2-7, Soft Cover

Lilah was six, almost 7. She liked school, reading, jumping on the trampoline in her back yard and playing with her hamster, Caramel.

On Monday,
Lilah's mom picked her up from school. "We need to stop by the store on the way home," said Mother. Lilah loved going to the store. There were so many things to see.

Clothes
Toys
Crafts
SHOES!
"Maybe Mom will let
me get a new pair
of shoes?"
thought Lilah.

Soon they arrived at the store and pulled their cart from the stack, laced together at the front door. Lilah's Mom pushed the cart, as Lilah bounced along beside her.

When they reached the Shoe Department, Lilah immediately grabbed a pair of shoes off the shelf. She tried on the blue shoes with an orange edge around the bottom.

Next, she tried the green shoes with the stars on the side.

Lilah turned and then she saw them-the perfect pair of shoes. She picked up the pink, glittery high-top tennis shoes, sat on the bench and tried them on. "Mom, oh Mom can I please get these shoes?"

"Lilah, sweetie, you have so many pairs of shoes. You don't even wear half of them and these shoes seem a little big." said Mother.

"Yes, but my princess shoes are already too small and they hurt and they're the wrong color . . . and . . . and . . .

Please!!!!!!

Finally, Mother gave in. "OK, but you must promise me you will wear these shoes and take good care of them."

"I promise," said Lilah, jumping around the shoe department.

Lilah was so excited about her new shoes. She wore her pink glittery shoes to school the next day and the day after that. All of Lilah's friends pointed at her glittery shoes and said how much they liked them. Lilah was very proud of her new shoes.

After a few days, the new-ness of Lilah's new shoes wore off. No one told her how cool her shoes were anymore. Lilah felt a little sad. She wished she could get another new pair of shoes, so her friends and teachers would notice but she knew her Mom would say no.

It was Friday and the sun was still shining bright as Lilah's Mom picked her up from school. Mother had to drop off some paperwork for her job and took a different way home. Lilah saw a park with a playground. "Mom, a playground. Can we go . . . please, please?"

"I guess so, just for a little while but you can't wear your new shoes on the playground? I put your old shoes in the car. You can wear those."
"But Mom,
I'd really like to wear
my new shoes."
"No, Lilah, you can go to the
playground only if you wear
your old shoes."

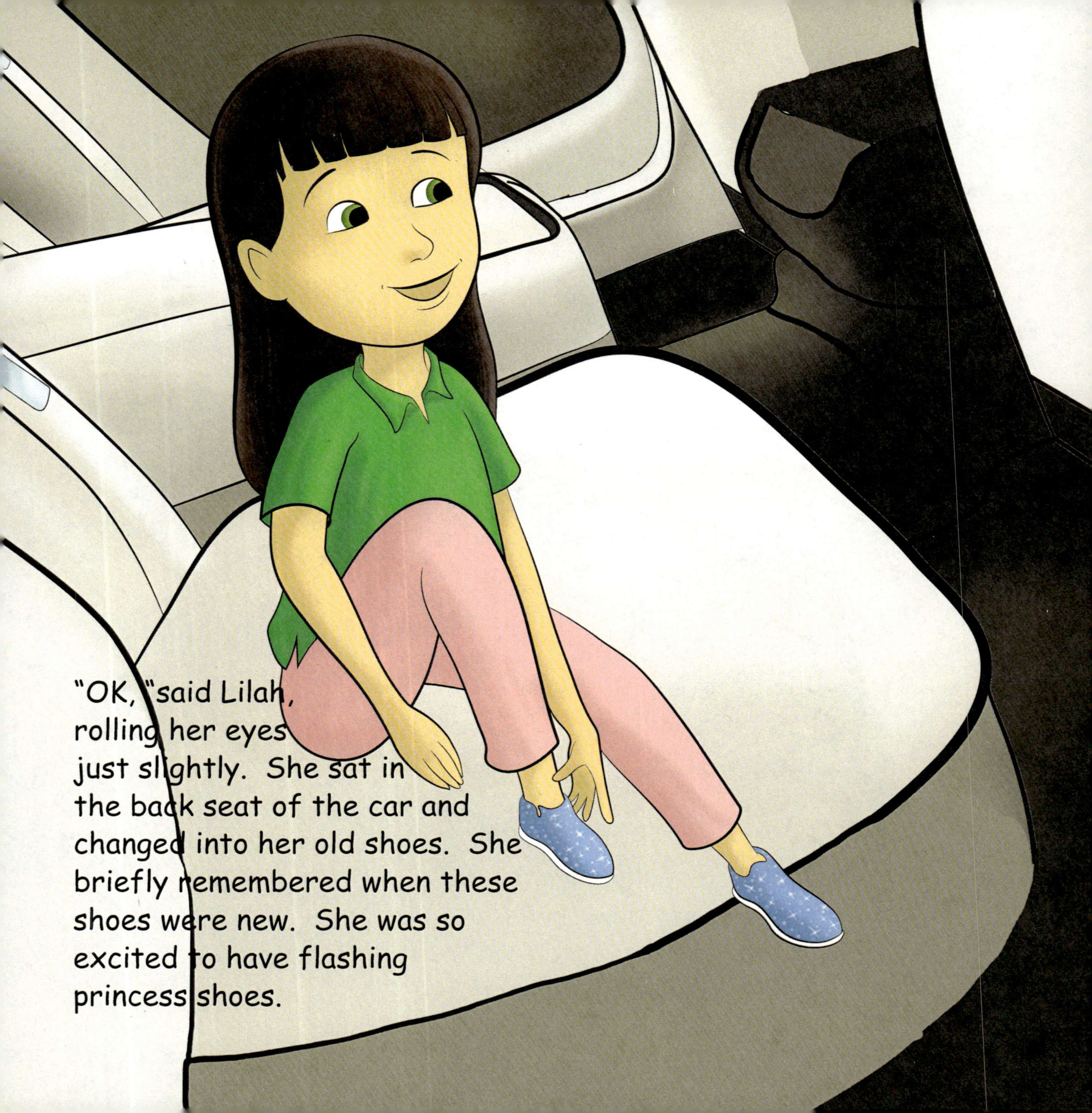

"OK, "said Lilah, rolling her eyes just slightly. She sat in the back seat of the car and changed into her old shoes. She briefly remembered when these shoes were new. She was so excited to have flashing princess shoes.

Lilah jumped from the car, took her Mom's hand and they walked to the playground.

For a short time, Lilah was one of only a few children playing, then two little girls broke free from their Mother and ran to edge of the playground.

The two girls looked a lot alike and Lilah thought they might be sisters. The taller girl seemed older than Lilah but the smaller girl was just about the same age. "Hi, what's your name," asked the smaller girl. "I'm Lilah. What's your name?" "I'm Violet and this is my big sister Allie."

The girls chased and laughed and went down the curvy slide again and again.

Violet pointed to Lilah's shoes. "You have the same shoes as me."

"What?" Lilah was feeling a little embarrassed about her old shoes. Then she looked at Violet's feet. The girls did have the same shoes. Violet's shoes were worn and the left one had a big scuff mark on the back. Lilah noticed when Violet ran up the stairs to the slide, the shoe on her right foot only flashed on one side.

"These were Allie's favorite shoes, then they got too small for her and she gave them to me. I was so excited to finally get these shoes," said Violet. "I love the princesses and the flashing when you step down. They are my favorite shoes," she said, as she raced to play in the sand pit.

Lilah felt a funny feeling in her stomach.

Lilah's shoes looked so much nicer than Violet's yet Lilah insisted that Mom buy her a new pair. She had only worn the new, pink glittery shoes for a week and was already hoping that mother would buy her another new pair of shoes.

Violet's shoes were worn and scuffed but it didn't matter. She laughed and played and loved her shoes.

The afternoon sun was beginning to fade. Lilah had so much fun with Violet and Allie and hoped she might see them again soon at the playground.

Monday came. Lilah got up, ate her breakfast, brushed her teeth, got dressed and ready for school. She started to put on her new, pink, glittery shoes, then she remembered her old princess shoes and ran to the car in the garage.

Lilah brushed off the dried mud, still caked on from the playground and put on the shoes. She stomped her feet and the shoes flashed. Lilah smiled. She remembered how happy these shoes had made her new friend, Violet and she felt happy too.

Since Lilah's new pink, glittery shoes were still a little big she'd have plenty of time to wear them, but for now she would wear her favorite flashing princess shoes!

The End

From Lillie: This book is dedicated to my favorite and only Mom, Tracie who has always taught me the importance of giving and the love of shoes. I love you more than anything. Happy Mother's Day,!

From Carol: This book is dedicated to my precious Tracie. You are an awesome Mom and inspiring woman. I am forever in awe of you. Thank you so much for giving me such incredible granddaughters and my adorable son-in-law. XOXO

SUSHI

Grow Grit Press

For school and book signings/readings, email marynhin@gmail.com
ISBN 978-1-951056-92-6
Cataloging in Publication Data Library of Congress Control number: 2019908171
Printed and bound in the USA. First printing June 2019
Free Coloring Pages at UnicornPreneur.com

Dedicated to our boys: Michael, Kobe, and Jojo.

May you follow your dreams wherever they may lead you.

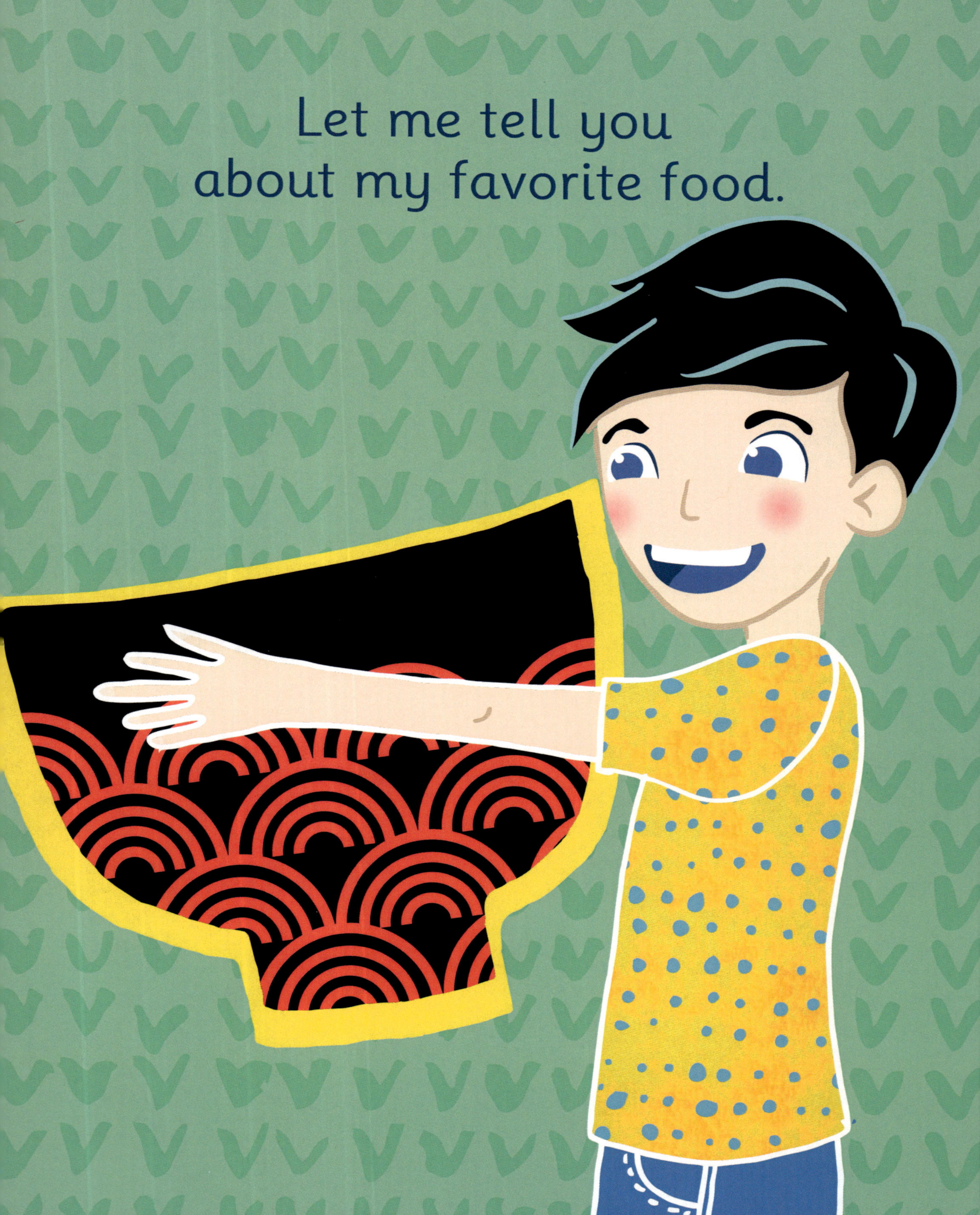
Let me tell you
about my favorite food.

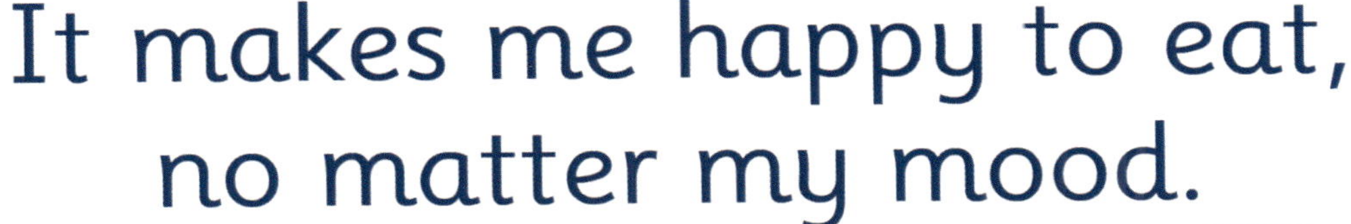

It makes me happy to eat,
no matter my mood.

It's a Japanese treat
that's so delicious.

Not only that,
it's pretty nutritious.

Have you guessed
it yet?
It's **SUSHI!**

In some parts of the world, it's called maki.

I eat it with fingers,
but you can use chopsticks
or a fork, too.

The bamboo mat used to roll sushi is called Makisu.

巻き簾

There are so many choices of rolls for sushi.

You can order a combo plate,
or just one if you're choosy.

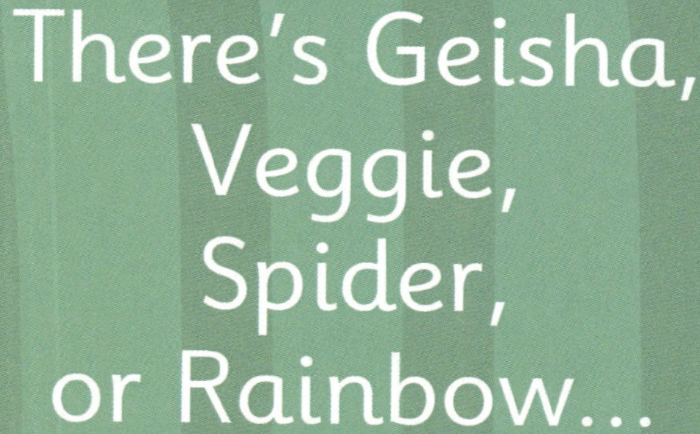

There's Geisha,
Veggie,
Spider,
or Rainbow...

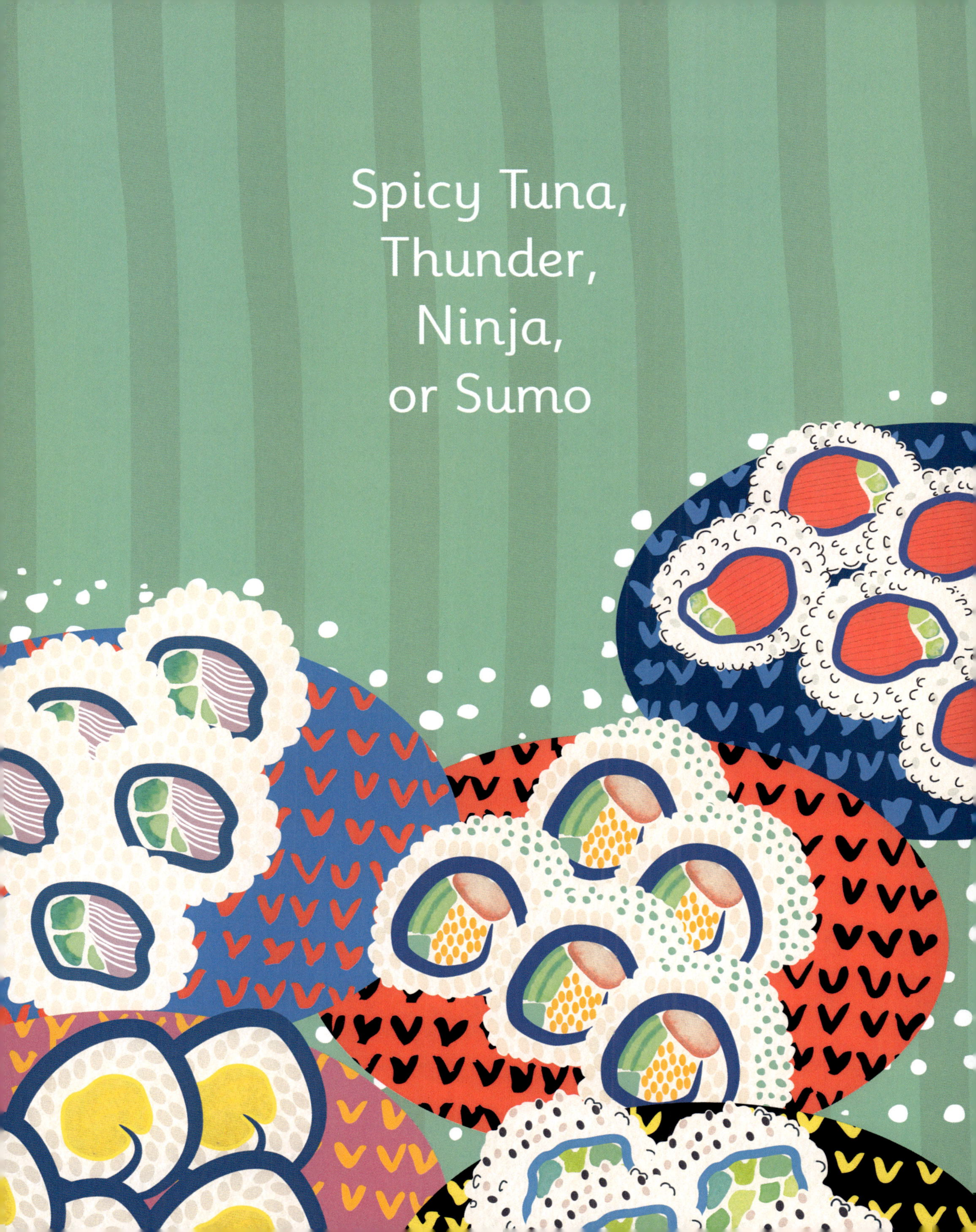

Spicy Tuna,
Thunder,
Ninja,
or Sumo

"California roll for me please,
miso soup on the side."

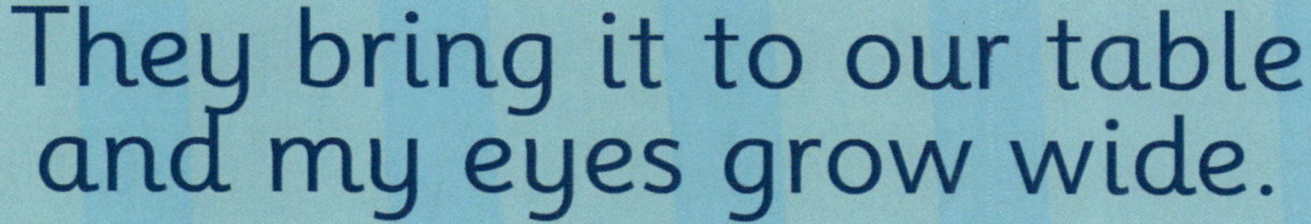
They bring it to our table
and my eyes grow wide.

Mom likes Tekka Maki,
a spicy tuna roll.

鉄火巻

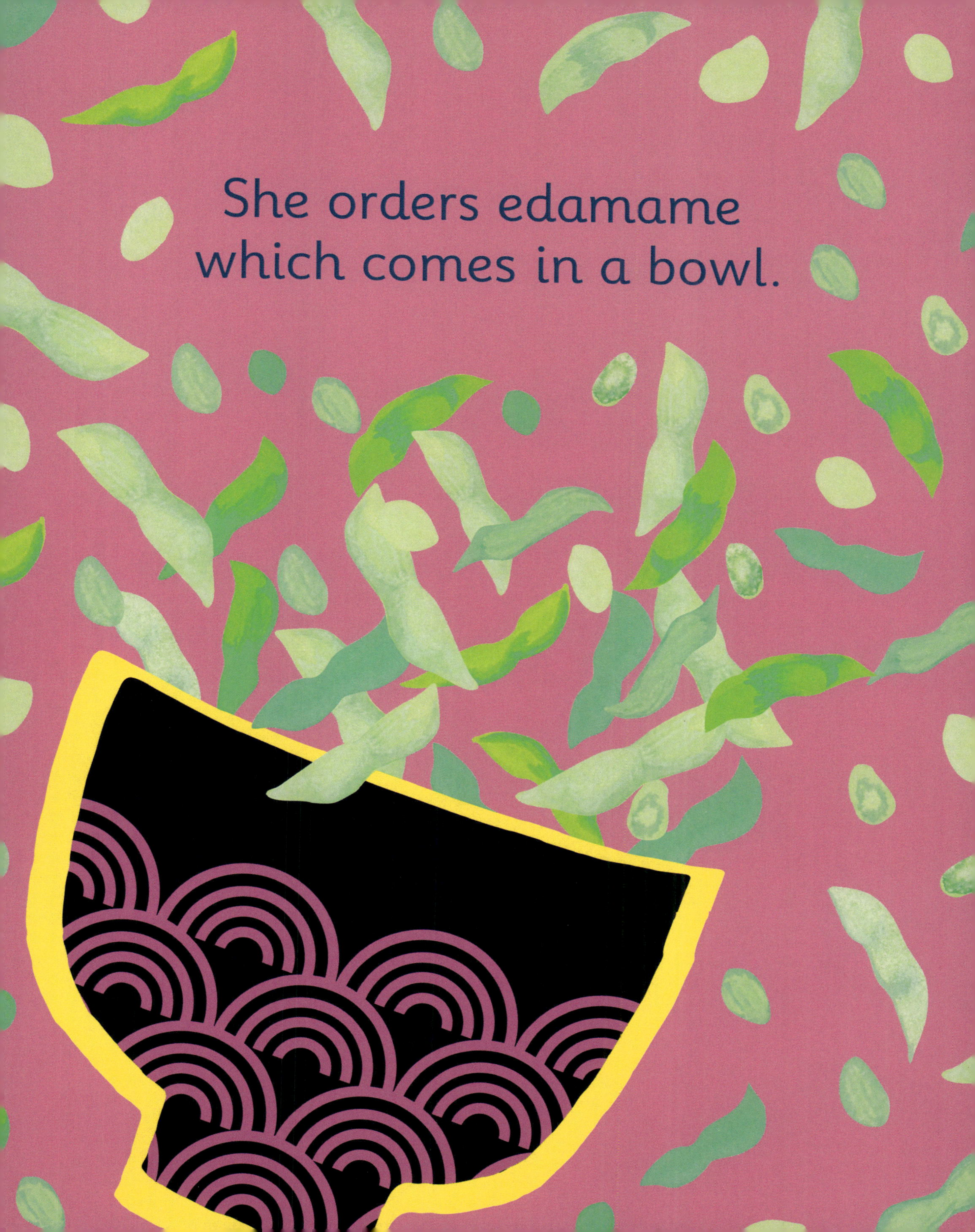

She orders edamame
which comes in a bowl.

Rolls come with fresh ginger
and wasabi that's HOT,

I love to eat sushi
with a special sauce that I got.

We eat it all up,
now our tummies are stuffed.

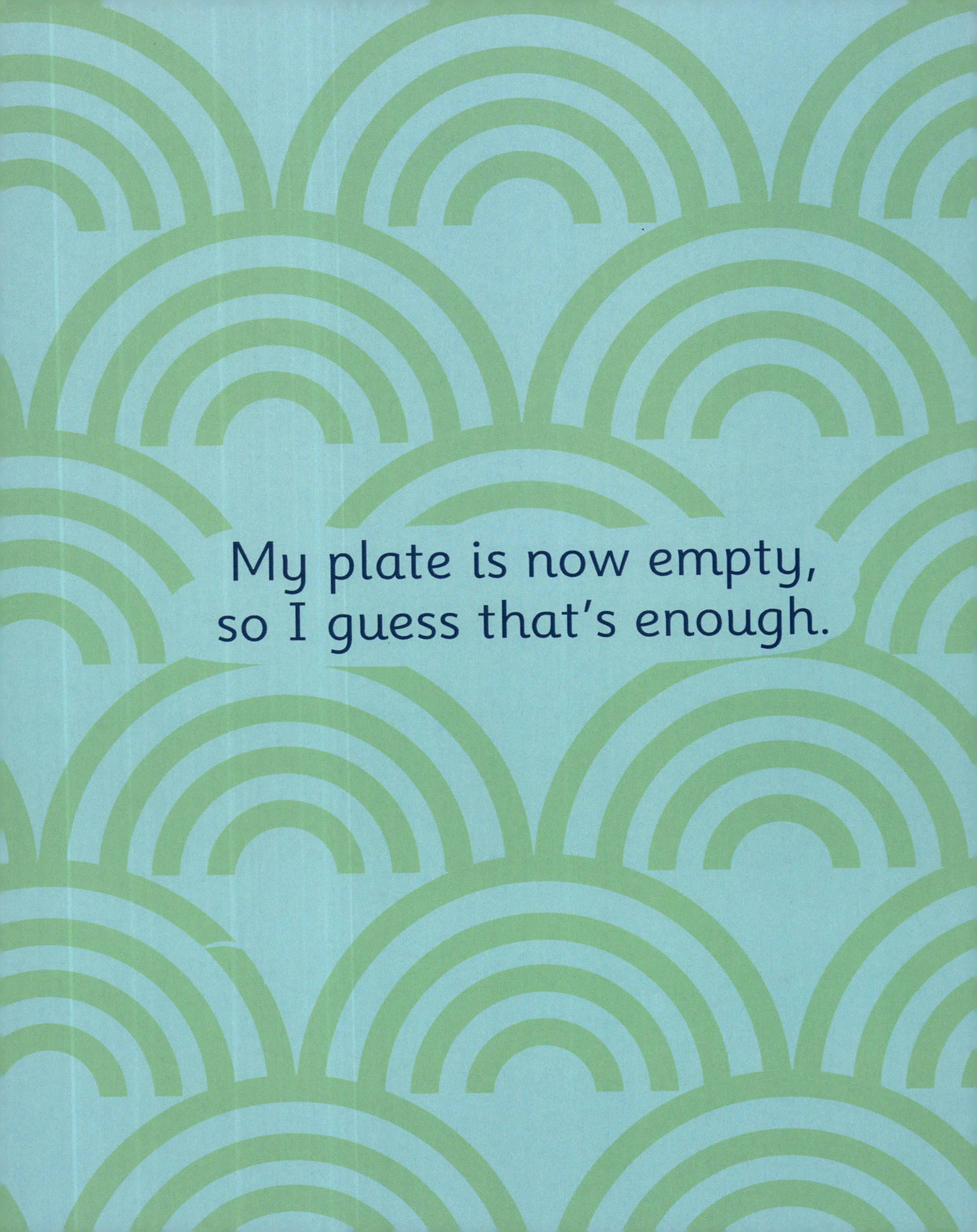

My plate is now empty,
so I guess that's enough.

Japanese Vocabulary

makisu
巻き簾

nori
海苔

Tekkamaki
鉄火巻

Maki
巻き寿司

Map of Japan and Japanese flag

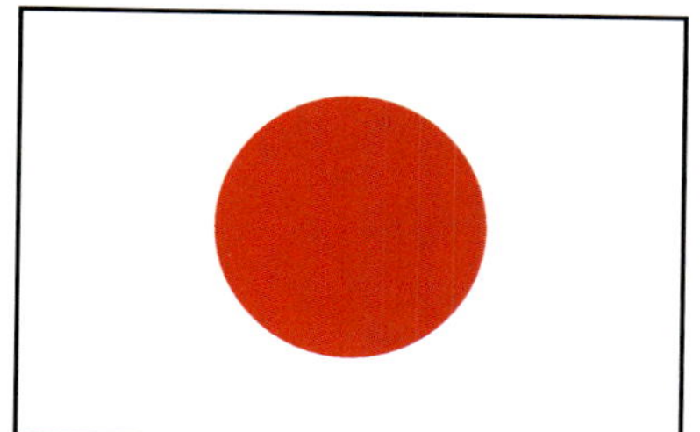

Can you find the country of Japan?

Interesting Facts About Sushi

- ✓ Not long ago, a sushi chefs had to undergo ten years of training before working in a restaurant. Today, demand for these skilled food artists is so high that many start work after only two years of training.

- ✓ The ginger served alongside your sushi is for you to clean your tongue's palate between bites and different fish.

- ✓ Japan's Agriculture Ministry has set up a panel to discuss a certification system for Japanese restaurants abroad. Possible gastronomic crimes include slicing fish too thick, using too little or too much wasabi and over-boiling rice.

- ✓ The highest price ever paid for a sushi grade Bluefin Tuna was $396,000 for a 754 pound fish ($526/lb) on January 4th, 2011 at the Tsukiji Fish Market in Tokyo. The United States Food and Drug Administration stipulates that all fish to be eaten raw (with the exception of tuna) must be frozen first, in order to kill parasites.

Fun DIY Sushi Craft

Materials:

- ✓ red, yellow, green felt
- ✓ Black masking tape or electrical tape or Washi tape
- ✓ cotton balls
- ✓ glue & scissors

Directions

1. Cut scraps of felt in fish or rectangular/diamond shapes.
2. Attach them to cotton balls with glue.
3. Wrap with black electrical tape.

Tag your photos @MaryNhin @GrowGrit to be featured in our marketing. If we use your picture, you'll receive our next book free!

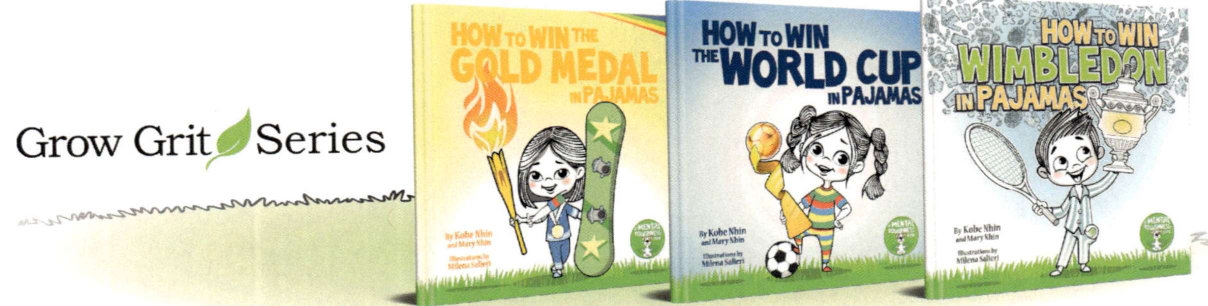

UnicornPreneur
Series

Made in the USA
Columbia, SC
02 August 2020

15272536R00022